# CONTRACT TO BUILD

Hawke House, the Headquarters of Higgins Group PLC

# CONTRACT TO BUILD

## THE D. J. HIGGINS STORY

Jonathan Mantle

JAMES
JAMES

© Higgins Group PLC

Hawke House
Old Station Road
Loughton
Essex IG10 4PE

First published 1994

ISBN 0907383 459

Designed by Bob Vickers

Published by
James & James (Publishers) Limited
Gordon House Business Centre
6 Lissenden Gardens
London NW5 ILX

# FOREWORD

THIS is a story about the Higgins family and their great adventure. It is a record of those exciting formative years and of our success which has been made possible by the commitment and forebearance of my wife Olive and our three sons.

George Eastwood gave devoted and loyal support which served as an example to all those who have followed.

My son, Stephen, and I have done our best to record accurately the achievements of the 'first generation'. In doing so we have attempted to pay tribute to all those who by their involvement have made this success story possible.

Before long it will be time for me to hand over to the next generation. Whatever happens I am confident that we shall continue our progress towards becoming one of the top national companies by the next millennium.

The policies which have served us so well as a family company will not change. The needs of our clients and the wellbeing of our staff are, and must always be, our first consideration.

DEREK HIGGINS
May 1994

# CONTENTS

Foreword   5

1   Building a Business   7

2   Into the Public Sector   24

3   21 Years On   33

4   Building a Greater London   40

5   Higgins Group PLC   45

Index   64

# Chapter One

# BUILDING A BUSINESS

On 1 March 1961 D. J. Higgins & Sons Limited was incorporated as a business. The directors were Derek Higgins, Olive Higgins and George Eastwood. Derek Higgins was 32 years old. His sons were four years, two years and nine months old respectively.

Both Derek Higgins and George Eastwood had given up well-paid jobs and had large young families. Britain was in a severe recession. At the best of times, the building trade had a high failure rate. D. J. Higgins & Sons Limited had no clients and no track record.

Today, Higgins Group PLC has an annual turnover of nearly £60 million. Higgins is a major contractor and developer in community and commercial building in Essex, Hertfordshire and Greater London. Derek Higgins and his three sons are all in the business.

The Higgins Group has weathered bad times and enjoyed prosperity. It has matured, especially in the last few years, into an organisation ready to flourish with the 1990s. Yet, an early client predicted that it had no more than 18 months to survive.

This is the story of why that prediction did not come true.

Derek Higgins did not come from a building background. His father was a lorry-driver and he lived with his parents at 21 High Road, Buckhurst Hill. He left Loughton School with no qualifications at the age of 16. In September 1945, he joined the local firm of Charles S. Foster & Sons, building contractors, as a junior clerk on 25s. a week, including alternate Saturday mornings.

After 15 months in the general office, they asked him if he would like to transfer to the estimating and surveying department. This involved the preparation of bills of quantities from drawings, measurements of work on various sites and estimating.

It also involved night school at the Building Department of the South West Essex Technical College. This enabled him to meet plasterers, bricklayers, carpenters and surveyors and make contacts which would stand him in good stead later. After studying for five years, three nights a week, he completed his apprenticeship. In 1951, he qualified as an Estimating Surveyor, passing the Licentiate examination of the Institute of Builders. He spent a year teaching quantity surveying at Walthamstow Technical College and worked for Foster & Sons as a site-based surveyor.

In 1952, Derek Higgins married Olive Pardey, who worked in the offices of the architects Tooley & Foster, where one of the surveyors was Derek's brother Bob. There was a great deal of work in these post-war years repairing bomb damage and new building. In 1953, he

Letter dated September 1945 appointing Derek Higgins to his first job – a junior clerk for a builder at 25s. per week.

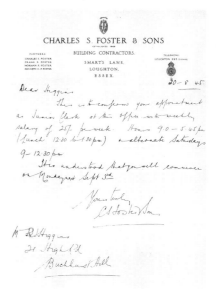

**W. & C. FRENCH**, LTD.,
CONTRACTORS FOR CIVIL ENGINEERING WORKS.

HEAD OFFICE:
BUCKHURST HILL,
ESSEX.

3 1 JUL 1960

Mr. D. J. Higgins

*Your Bank Account has today been credited with the undermentioned amount, made up as follows :—*

| | | |
|---|---|---|
| Salary for the month | ... ... | £113.15 |
| Subsistence Allowance | ... ... | : : |
| Car Allowance | ... ... | : : |
| | | £113.15 |

LESS

| | | |
|---|---|---|
| National Insurance £ | 1:19:8 | |
| Income Tax (Code No. 138) | 12.4 | |
| Superannuation | 4:11 | £18:14:8 |
| Amount of Credit | | £95 : :4 |

FOR AND ON BEHALF OF

**W. & C. FRENCH, LTD.**
E. C. BOTTING,

*Accountant.*

WCF/61  CP 6316

A pay slip showing Derek Higgins's gross pay at W. & C. French Limited, July 1960, as £113 15s. per month.

decided to look farther afield than Essex. The bigger firms separated the functions of estimator and surveyor and he became a pure estimator with the inner-London based firm of Gee Walker & Slater Limited.

He worked there for a year, and spent a couple of weeks on their behalf in Cyprus. The senior estimator, Bill Davies, became a lifelong friend: 'One day,' he told him, 'you'll be earning a thousand a year!'

After a year with Gee Walker & Slater, he returned to Essex to the firm of W. & C. French Limited in Buckhurst Hill. He stayed with the firm from 1954 until 1961. His father had died in 1953.

In 1960, his mother died and left him a modest legacy. One day that same year, he walked into his office, which he shared with a surveyor called George Eastwood.

'I'm going to start up on my own in building,' he told him.

Eastwood's reaction was immediate: 'I'll come with you,' he said.

They left behind Robert Webster, the chief estimator, and Michael Bull, an estimator who had been one of Higgins's pupils at the Technical College. Years later, Webster would retire and join Higgins and Eastwood as part-time estimator at their offices in Horn Lane. In May 1986, his son Colin Webster became a non-executive director of D. J. Higgins & Sons Limited until his retirement.

Michael Bull went on to become chief estimator for French Kier at their Witham Branch.

One of Derek Higgins's many tenders for W. & C. French had been the new Daily Mirror headquarters in High Holborn, which he priced in 1956 under the direction of Col. Charles Newman VC. The site-based surveyor was Brian Hamilton, destined to join D. J. Higgins & Sons in May 1986 as their surveying director.

The two men gave W. & C. French six months' notice. Their boss, Col. Sir Arthur Noble, was sorry to see them go.

So was Mr Tucker, Derek Higgins's bank manager. 'You are mad,' he said, when Derek Higgins told him he was setting up in business and leaving a perfectly good job and salary, 'You are mad,' he repeated, 'and I will not support you. Builders have the highest bankruptcy rate, and it will be years before you get back to earning a decent salary.'

Derek Higgins was dismayed at this and reported as much to Attwater & Lyle, the solicitors who advised him at the time. They introduced him to Gerald Birch, manager of the local branch of the Midland Bank, where W. & C. French had their accounts.

Mr Birch gave Derek Higgins a warm welcome, and would become a trusted friend over the years.

Derek Higgins went back to Mr Tucker. 'I am moving up the road to the Midland,' he told him.

'And I still won't help you,' was the reply.

Higgins and Eastwood had discussed the name of the new business and rejected the joint title. Derek Higgins was particularly hopeful that his young sons would join him in time. D. J. Higgins & Sons Limited was incorporated. On the letterhead it said simply 'Builders.'

They needed premises. 173 Horn Lane, Woodford Green, Essex was up for sale at auction. It had only three bedrooms, was badly heated, and was by the railway, but it had a yard and a large shed suitable for plant and materials. Derek Higgins sold the Higgins family's comfortable four-bedroom house in Roebuck Lane, Buckhurst Hill, and his new Ford Consul, and bought the house and yard and a Ford 500E van which they painted red in the new firm's colours. Derek and Olive Higgins and their three sons, Richard, Stephen and Martin, moved into 173 Horn Lane in September 1960.

George Eastwood, who had five children, remained living where he was. But on leaving W. & C. French he had to return his company car. He purchased a bicycle.

D. J. Higgins & Sons Limited designed and built its first job at the back of 173 Horn Lane . This was a small single-storey office with a lean-to roof, made of blocks and asbestos. They furnished it with second-hand desks, chairs and a telephone.

Derek Higgins sat at one side and George Eastwood sat at the other. Olive Higgins, when she was not looking after the three children, took care of the typing and the accounts and sat in the middle.

The company took on its first employee. Bill Pardey, Derek Higgins's father-in-law, was a First World War veteran and painter and decorator. At 67, he was already two years past the age of retirement, but he was keen to work and could turn his hand to plumbing.

The new company had premises, transport, plant and enthusiasm. It also had a motto: 'The client is right and we do not fall out with anyone.' Unfortunately, as yet, it did not have any clients, and thus did not

WOODFORD GREEN - ESSEX.

THE EXCELLENT
FREEHOLD DWELLING HOUSE AND
BUILDER'S YARD
173, HORN LANE
comprising:—
THE FREEHOLD DWELLING HOUSE
of substantial construction with good brick elevations and a blue slate roof and having
the following accommodation:—
Three Good Size Bedrooms      Landing, Bathroom, W.C.
Spacious Entrance Hall.   Large Living Room.   Excellent Kitchen Quarters
and Pleasant Small Garden.
THE EXTENSIVE BUILDER'S YARD
approached through a covered entrance enclosed by double gates and leading to a large
yard upon which are constructed:—
A Large Joiner's Shop.      General Store and Extensive Timber Storage.
SELF CONTAINED OFFICE
Having a separate street entrance and an interior access to the living accommodation.
(The premises have an existing user as a Builder's Yard.)
Will be sold by Auction with
VACANT POSSESSION
by FREDERICK H.

# WORLEY

(Unless sold previously by private treaty)
at
The "Eagle" Hotel, Snaresbrook, E.11,
on
WEDNESDAY, 21st SEPTEMBER, 1960,
at 6.30 p.m.

Particulars and Conditions of Sale of :-            The Auctioneers,
           The Solicitors,                   Westminster Bank Buildings,
Messrs. Leaser, Fairbank & Co.,         114, George Lane, Woodford, E.18.
1 & 2, St. George Street, Hanover Square, W.1.   Tel.: WANstead 0428 and 0694.
        MAYfair 6131 (3 lines).          And 16, The Broadway, Woodford Green.
      And at Barkingside, Essex.              Tel.: BUCkhurst 5783.

Derek and Olive Higgins bought 173 Horn Lane at the auction announced here (above). It was to serve as the company's first premises – and the Higgins family's home – for many years.

*Below left:* The office and section of the yard at Horn Lane.

*Below right:* George Eastwood (right) and Richard Higgins with the company's first van, a red Ford 500E in the firm's colours, 1961.

have the chance to test out its motto. But, over 30 years later, Derek Higgins would still remember the unique sensation when he and George Eastwood started trading:

'I cannot explain to you the excitement, the thrill, of those formative years. Going out to work in that office with this wonderful man, who was and still is my closest friend.'

D. J. Higgins & Sons Limited priced and won its first job on 8 March 1961. This was to decorate ceilings for a Miss Leonard of Nesta Road, Woodford Green. The job was worth £36. 10s. 0d.

Derek Higgins and his father-in-law carried out the work. George Eastwood, who had progressed to the status of surveyor by way of being a carpenter and general foreman, was meanwhile dispatched to repair a tenanted house owned by Derek Higgins's brother Bob in Roding Lane, Buckhurst Hill.

With few clients and no track record, the work came in slowly. Many promises of work never materialised. The recession made matters worse. One of their early clients was himself a subcontractor.

'You won't last 18 months,' he said; and such was his despair that 18 months later he was gone, while they were still there. But the early going was hard. They had both left comparatively well-paid jobs to become workmen, and apart from groundwork, such as digging trenches, they did not turn anything down. Eastwood, the more accomplished craftsman, was a less experienced decorator who liked to stand back every so often and admire his handiwork. This always provoked a withering remark from Derek Higgins's father-in-law, Bill Pardey 'Of course, you always were slow on the brush, weren't you, George?' he used to say.

On one occasion they failed to win the job of painting a petrol station, but were hired to clean it instead. Derek Higgins was wiping down the pumps on the forecourt, when a woman pulled up in a Rolls-Royce and tapped on the windscreen.

At first he ignored her, but then realised she wanted him to clean it too. Some years later he would have a Rolls-Royce of his own, but meanwhile he cleaned it for her. When he had finished she gave him 2s., which he pocketed and later gave to his father-in-law.

Gradually, the scores of small domestic jobs they priced each month turned into commissions. They decorated inside and outside, repaired roofs and drains and garden walls and repointed chimney-stacks. They found a place on the list of approved jobbing builders – they were not yet regarded as fully fledged contractors – of Essex County Council.

The first job for the Council was to install new drainage for Wanstead County High School. It was worth £59. 10s. 0d. This was followed by more jobs of the same kind for which they tendered, although not always successfully: 'Lowest but not accepted!' read the Estimate Book for 30 May 1962, for a tender of £31,197 for 24 flats for Ilford Borough Council; a little optimistic, perhaps, for the company at the time. But the growing number of local authority tenders in which they were successful, enabled them to widen their activities from the purely domestic to the public sector; and the public sector was where Derek Higgins very much wanted D. J. Higgins & Sons Limited to be.

Eighteen months after they started trading they were still in business. They had turned over £9,705. 9s. 0d. in their first year and made a profit of £58. 4s. 4d.

Olive Higgins was able to hand over her secretarial work in the office to Gladys Smith, who had been George Eastwood's secretary at W. & C. French. Gladys became a much-loved and greatly respected member of the company and would remain with D. J. Higgins & Sons Limited for the rest of her life.

The first marketing effort for the company came about literally by accident. A carpenter on the books called Bill Longley severed the tops of his fingers while planing in the shed in the yard on a Universal woodworking machine. Unable to work as a carpenter, he was dispatched to deliver hundreds of leaflets advertising the new company's services through the letter-boxes of the locality.

The winter of 1962-63 was the worst in living memory. In the Higgins' house at Horn Lane a bottle of camphorated oil froze solid on a dressing-table; no amount of roaring fires made a difference and there was no central heating. When a relation commissioned them to build an office in the hangar-roof at Stapleford Aerodrome, Derek Higgins and George Eastwood were relieved at the prospect of working under cover.

## D. J. HIGGINS & SONS LIMITED
### BUILDERS
**173 Horn Lane, Woodford Green, Essex**
BUC 2249

We offer a competitive and efficient service in any of the following, let us quote you for your requirements, your enquiries will be dealt with quickly and remember all items of expenditure on repairs and maintenance qualify for relief under Schedule 'A' Tax.

Interior and exterior decorations.

Complete modernisation of your kitchen or bathroom.

Is your loft insulated? Let us fit Fibreglass insulation and save fuel costs.

We will design and submit plans to the Local Authority for your new garage, or any extensions you may require.

Why not have that old fence removed? We will construct new brick boundary walls complete with ornamental iron gates.

Are your garden paths and garage runway dilapidated? Coloured tarmacadam is durable, inexpensive and attractive to look at, let us advise you.

Do you need purpose-made fitments in your kitchen or bedrooms? We are fully equipped to provide built-in wardrobes, cupboards, sink units, formica work-tops etc.

**PLEASE CONTACT US BY TELEPHONE FOR AN APPOINT-MENT DURING WEEKDAY, EVENING OR WEEKEND**

The company's first marketing effort.

An early estimate. The tender was successful.

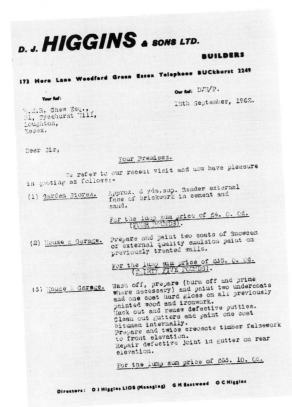

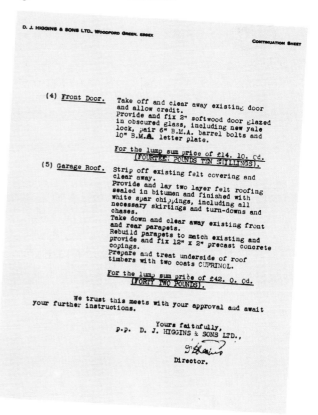

The house at Horn Lane which accommodated the Higgins family and, later, the company offices.

A few weeks later, stepping back to admire his work as usual, Eastwood fell 13 feet and broke a wrist and an ankle. Eastwood was unable to work for weeks and Derek Higgins visited him each night on his way home.

Years later, in a speech on the company's twenty-first anniversary, Derek Higgins would jokingly suggest that the accident was a ploy on the other man's part to escape the rigours of that winter. At the time,

Rear view of Horn Lane showing the offices and yard. The sign 'D. J. Higgins & Sons Ltd' may be discerned on the side of the house.

however, his concern for his friend was also for practical reasons. Higgins, left working on his own in the hangar, was anxious about his ability to install a tricky piece of flashing on a gable. Eastwood, laid up in bed, supplied him with a drawing that enabled him to finish the job.

In spite of the hard winter, in their second trading year D. J. Higgins & Sons Limited turned over £40,000 and increased their profits.

Derek Higgins stopped manual work and concentrated on pricing and ordering for jobs which either he or George Eastwood ran. The injured carpenter resumed his duties. Painters and decorators came and went in increasing numbers and Bill Pardey continued to be the business's first and oldest employee.

The Higgins family lived in the house, and their pet rabbit lived in the front garden. In the office, Gladys Smith oversaw accounts and salaries which reflected the growing turnover: exterior decorating, garage extensions, concrete paving, roofs, gutters, central heating, shop interiors. The clients, as well as private individuals, included the Midland Bank, East Barnet Urban District Council, the Metropolitan Police and J. Sainsbury Limited.

At his branch of the Midland Bank, Mr Birch was justifiably pleased.

When Ron Hatch joined in April 1964, the orders for new building work at last began to arrive. Essex County Council was prepared to give D. J. Higgins & Sons Limited an opportunity, and this meant taking on their first general foreman. Ron Hatch was chosen, and his first contract was to build a pair of houses at Brentwood under the critical eye of George Eastwood. In 1989, Ron Hatch was to celebrate 25 years' service, and after taking early retirement in 1990 he continued to work as holiday relief for the company.

In the third year, the turnover tripled to £120,000. The technique of tendering low for as many jobs as possible and undercutting others was financed by this rapid growth and by the policy of the directors of only working for wages. The volume and quality of the work were sustained by the long hours worked by Derek Higgins and George Eastwood, and by the growing number of skilled craftsmen and subcontractors willing to work for D. J. Higgins & Sons.

The office they had built at the back of 173 Horn Lane was no longer big enough, and the Higgins family moved out to a house they purchased five minutes away. The grass was concreted over where the rabbit had grazed and the first floor was let for a time to an electrical company. The ground floor of 173 Horn Lane became the business premises of D. J. Higgins & Sons.

The number and size of the contracts continued to grow. The company renovated a public library in Wanstead, a state boarding school in Fyfield, a Roman Catholic day school in Basildon, and police houses in Forest Gate. The public sector construction contracts for which they tendered aggressively continued to elude them, but they

Stephen, Richard and Martin Higgins (from left to right), standing in the company's first lorry, 1963.

continued to win many private industrial jobs individually worth thousands of pounds.

In March 1965, D. J. Higgins Developments Limited was incorporated. The purchase of land and development of higher-quality housing was a growing phenomenon in the economic climate of the middle 1960s. Profit margins on pure building were safe but low, and development offered a source of profits to an ambitious builder whose tenders were routinely submitted on a near-cost-only basis.

D. J. Higgins & Sons had successfully used its rising turnover to finance its low tenders and undercut competitors. As long as turnover continued to cover costs, the strategy could be said to be working. But costs could rise without warning and in ways that were impossible to control. As Derek Higgins would discover, even in a stable climate, there was a difference between becoming a successful developer and running a successful building company.

In 1966, the company ran into precisely these problems. The cost of the building business exceeded the turnover, the amount of new business declined, and the new development business failed to provide profits. After five years in business, it looked as though the predictions of the subcontractor in the early 1960s were belatedly about to come true.

Later, Derek Higgins and George Eastwood would reflect on the factors that so nearly brought them to grief. They would realise they had been given one opportunity, and one alone, to learn a lesson they should never forget.

'When we started in business,' Derek Higgins recalled, 'I wanted to start from the bottom. A lot of people fail because they start half-way up. I wanted to start with the lowest possible overheads, and work up.'

They realised that they had departed from this founding principle. Costs had risen out of control and creditors were beginning to press. On Black Monday, as they called it afterwards, they called various employees into the office and told them with great regret that their services were no longer required. Of the main permanent staff, only Derek Higgins, George Eastwood and Gladys Smith remained.

The savings they made that day in wages and the two company cars saved the company

'It was a bitter pill, after five years,' George Eastwood recalled, 'but this was also our strength, that we could shrink back to just the two of us. We knew we could do it ourselves, because we had started out like that. And we had come a long way as businessmen.'

'It's a great business from the point of view of turnover,' Derek Higgins recalled, 'You can survive a long time on that, especially if you are expanding as we were. But if you don't eventually make a profit, you will go broke. So we learned from 1966, and we pulled the business back.'

D. J. Higgins & Sons Limited had expanded its turnover spectacularly in only a few years. This had suddenly been enough to threaten the business. There would be difficult times ahead, some of them encountered in the course of attempting to make a profit. But the importance of making a profit, above all else, would never be forgotten again.

Throughout the second half of the 1960s, D. J. Higgins & Sons increased the number and size of its jobs in the public sector and concentrated on keeping its overheads as low as its tenders. Derek Higgins and George Eastwood routinely worked 14 hours a day, pricing and ordering for jobs in housing, schools, and hospitals. Cricket was their only relaxation.

They played midweek cricket on Thursday afternoons for Liverpool Victoria. Eastwood was an accomplished opening batsman and Higgins a useful all-rounder.

Derek Higgins nursed a burning ambition to play on the top ground at Buckhurst Hill. At last the great day came when he and Eastwood were chosen to open the batting for South Loughton.

The sun shone; the sky was blue; Eastwood faced the first ball.

He played it to the covers and shouted to Higgins: 'Run!'

Higgins ran, and was run out first ball. Higgins and Eastwood later moved on to other clubs and experienced considerable success in their

Elderly Persons' Home, Canvey Island. Completed in 1966, it was then by far the largest job Higgins had undertaken and marked a quantum change in the scale of the business.

Little Heath ESN School, Ilford, 1969 (Client and Architect: London Borough of Redbridge).

different ways. But Higgins never forgot what happened on the top ground at Buckhurst Hill, and never played there again.`

The sporting connection proved more fruitful when the return to profitability made it necessary to bring on board another director.

Gordon Bent knew George Eastwood through Wanstead Cricket Club. Bent's father was a builder and the family business of H. Bent & Co. was over 100 years old.

In 1965, Gordon Bent had left his father and started his own business. By 1969, D. J. Higgins & Sons was turning over £330,000 a year. Bent was only half serious when he remarked to George Eastwood that he had seen a newspaper advertisement by Higgins for the position of senior manager, and wondered if he should apply.

The arrival of Gordon Bent at Horn Lane relieved the strain on Derek Higgins and George Eastwood and proved a fruitful association for all parties. Bent became manager of the Small Works Department and took overall charge of the yard, transport, plant and stock.

Gordon Bent was still running a number of contracts and possessed a certain amount of plant, which he made available to D. J. Higgins and Sons. He was formally invited to join the board of D. J. Higgins & Sons in 1971.

In 1970, the company took on more foremen, supervisors and surveyors and successfully tendered for its largest contract to date. This

*Right:* The last photograph of 173 Horn Lane just before the company moved out in 1987; it was then demolished and redeveloped. The original storage building, with flag, is at the rear.

was to build the Cornelius Vermuyden Comprehensive School on Canvey Island for Essex County Council and was worth £320,000, a massive sum.

The foreman for the job, Leslie Toomer, had started with D. J. Higgins & Sons as a carpenter at 8s. 3d. an hour. He would retire in 1993 after 25 years' service, and continue to remain active working holiday relief for the company. Leslie Toomer, Ron Hatch, Tony Collins and Jim Oliff were all skilled former tradesmen who became

*Continued on page 23*

Mitchell Junior School, Hornchurch.

Newtons Junior School, Rainham,
1969 (Client and Architect:
London Borough of Havering).

Richard's Place, flats in London E17, 1985 (Client: London Borough of
Waltham Forest).

Limewood Court, Ilford, the first sheltered housing scheme by D. J. Higgins Developments Limited, 1990 (Architect: Carr Goldsmith & Fallek).

*Opposite:* Office building, Bartholomew Close, in the City of London, 1989 (Client: Metro Properties Limited; Architect: Green Lloyd).

*Above:* Pickford's Wharf, opened 1990 (Client and Architect: London Borough of Islington). (See page 49).

*Left:* Office block, South Street, Romford, developed and built by Higgins, 1990, was later occupied by Polygram UK Limited (Client: Higgins Group PLC; Architect: Eric Askew).

general foremen with the company during these years, and spent the rest of their working lives with the company.

The Canvey Island contract was the biggest of a string of big public sector contracts. These also included Rainham Secondary School (£220,000) for the London Borough of Havering, Farnham Road School (£120,000) for the London Borough of Redbridge and Harlow ESN School, as it was then known, (£80,000) for Essex County Council.

At the end of its first ten years of trading, D. J. Higgins & Sons Limited had come a long way from the days of two men, a van and a bicycle. It had enjoyed early growth, weathered sudden crisis and recovered to penetrate the higher levels of the public sector in Essex, Hertfordshire and Greater London. The first half of the 1970s would see further growth in the contracting business and attempts at development; and in an economic climate even more volatile than that of the decade that had gone before.

## Chapter Two

# INTO THE PUBLIC SECTOR

In 1971, Don Price joined D. J. Higgins & Sons Limited as buyer, dealing with materials and subcontractors, and eventually took over as chief estimator. Both were demanding jobs which Derek Higgins himself had handled for many years. Derek Higgins had known Don Price at night school, and Price had later worked with Higgins and Eastwood at W. & C. French Limited in Buckhurst Hill.

The Canvey Island contract greatly strengthened the position of the company in the public and community sector. Recent successful tenders were worth hundreds of thousands of pounds and included schools in Barnet, Tilbury, Mill Hill, East Ham, Hackney, Hawkwell and Walthamstow, as well as a police station in Romford and a Jewish Youth Centre in Redbridge.

The number and size of new contracts began to place a strain on the resources of the company. A search was under way for a larger office and yard but this had so far been unsuccessful. There was also a shortage of reliable tradesmen and labourers, and staff were encouraged to bring possible candidates along to Horn Lane.

The stream of contracts for schools, sports clubs, office buildings and synagogues continued into 1972. Derek Higgins was also

Brady Junior School, Rainham, 1969.

ambitious to extend the activities of D. J. Higgins Developments Limited, which had begun by building a single detached house in Stag Lane, Buckhurst Hill. Staff were encouraged to look out for potential sites and old houses ripe for purchase.

But when D. J. Higgins Developments Limited built a terrace of three-bedroom houses on land it had purchased at the rear of the Two Brewers in Chigwell Row, it discovered that what had been intended as a low-cost housing development was nothing of the kind. A sudden deepening recession threw out all the careful cost calculations of land, building work, planning and bank interest and any hope of profits.

Unable to sell on the open market, the company was forced to cut its losses and sell the completed development to Chigwell Urban District Council.

As George Eastwood recalled: 'Something had to be done, and we did it. It happens to everyone in this business.'

Derek Higgins agreed: 'We took a pounding, but we sold them. Move on. It's never wrong to sell.'

None the less, the experience and the deepening recession were enough to persuade D. J. Higgins Developments Limited to turn its back for the time being on the so-called 'cheaper' end of the market.

The worsening British economic situation in the early 1970s did not immediately make itself felt in the public sector. Budgets for the type of contracts for which the company tendered were set a long time in advance. Local authority spending programmes represented major investments made for social and environmental as well as economic reasons.

D. J. Higgins & Sons Limited responded to the growing volume of work by building up its own labour force. This meant the company could pay wage increases direct and reduce its dependence on labour-only subcontractors.

It also took greater care not to overload the subcontractors it did employ: 'It's not cheap,' Derek Higgins liked to remind staff, 'if you can't get it.'

But in its zeal to improve services for citizens from the cradle to the grave, the public sector too looked for value for money in the contractors it chose to construct its schools, old peoples homes and health centres. The company could not afford to take for granted the position it had built up in this market. There was no doubt that its ability to tender very competitively and still make a profit would be tested to the full, if D. J. Higgins & Sons Limited was to trade through yet another downturn in the economic climate.

In 1973, the company won its largest contract to date for £468,000 to build old persons' flatlets in Cathall Road for the London Borough of Waltham Forest. Tony Collins was the site agent. Collins had served his apprenticeship as a carpenter and joiner in the late 1950s in the yard at Horn Lane, when working for A. R. Sheppard, a firm of builders.

As the recession deepened and brought with it the energy crisis, fuel rationing and the three-day week, D. J. Higgins & Sons Limited continued to grow and look for larger premises to house its offices and plant.

In 1974, the company won the contract for £584,000 to build an extension to the King Harold Secondary School at Waltham Abbey for Essex County Council. Jim Oliff had joined the company in 1968 as a site agent and was entrusted with this major project. Oliff was to receive his long service award in the boardroom on 10 November 1993. His assistant in those days, former carpenter Arthur Coe, had joined in 1967, and he too would still be with the company in 1994.

This was a far cry from the first contract the company had won to install new drainage for £59.10s. 0d., for the same client just over a decade earlier.

Great Baddow Comprehensive School was another contract won from Essex County Council at this time by D. J. Higgins & Sons Limited, and the first to employ one of the sons.

Richard Higgins joined the company in April 1974 as a junior surveyor on a day release scheme. Under the supervision of Terry Edwards, a trained surveyor who visited the site regularly, he learned to measure work, pay subcontractors and help with the monthly valuations. After a while, he was sent to the King Harold Secondary School site at Waltham Abbey, also under the supervision of Edwards, to further his experience there.

1975 saw D. J. Higgins & Sons Limited ease its overcrowding problem by acquiring premises for its Plant Department at Cowslip Road, South Woodford. The main office at Horn Lane was extended but the volume of business was such that more space was still needed.

The new building works department under Gordon Bent dealt mainly with rehabilitation work, and this and the contracting company generally was flourishing in spite of the continued economic crisis in the country as a whole. The contract of £897,000 for the rehabilitation of houses for Islington Council, was the largest yet in a series of successful tenders that included an infants' school in Chingford, a primary school in Poplar, a secondary school in Woodford Green, and an old people's home in Walthamstow.

1975 was also D. J. Higgins & Sons Limited's fifteenth year of trading and the company produced an illustrated brochure to enlighten staff and the rest of the world about its activities. The staff held their first dinner dance, subsidised by the directors, and 120 people attended. Prompted by the new Health and Safety at Work Act, the company also purchased a 16mm projector and seven safety films to show on sites to employees at the different stages of the construction process.

Football matches took place between contract staff and staff from Horn Lane, and Derek Higgins and George Eastwood remained active in the sporting scene. Derek Higgins had played hockey since his schooldays and in 1977 would be elected Captain of the Old

Science Block, Rainham Secondary School, one of many system-built schools constructed by Higgins in the 1970s (Client and Architect: London Borough of Havering).

Swimming-pool, Rainham Secondary School.

Loughtonians Hockey Club and Captain of Matching Green Cricket Club. George Eastwood, finding his eyesight was no longer sufficient to face fast bowling, gave up cricket for race walking and running with Woodford Green Athletic Club. Typically, he would go on to compete in marathons and win medals in veterans' events around the world.

*

New contract values by this time were routinely in six figures and the combined annual turnover of D. J. Higgins & Sons Limited and D. J. Higgins Developments Limited rose from £3.75 million in 1975–6 to over £5 million in 1976–7. The rehabilitation and new building areas of the business grew and new professional and clerical staff were taken on. Among these was Barry Penman, who joined full time in 1976 as chief surveyor, having consulted to the company for some time in this capacity.

D. J. Higgins & Sons Limited had just won its first £1 million contract from the B'Nai Brith Housing Association to build a hostel and flatlets at 99 Princes Park Avenue, Golders Green. Jim Mutter, another new arrival at the company, was assigned to the contract as a buyer.

Mutter had had job offers from several contractors larger than Higgins. But at his interview he was impressed with the way Derek Higgins identified buying, traditionally regarded an essential but unglamorous occupation, as a crucial part of the business. Mutter liked what he saw and felt this was a company in which he could make a career. Nearly 20 years later, he would be on the board of D. J. Higgins & Sons Limited, so his initial instincts were correct.

Mutter set to work with just one youthful assistant. After a ten hour day he would frequently go home, help put the children to bed, and then work again from 10 p.m. to midnight. He had no budget as such, but had to buy against targets, and every so often he would receive a call from Derek Higgins asking him to 'explain' why he had made a particular decision. Once, he was badly caught out, as buyers can be; he never let it happen again.

After a few months, Mutter decided to sit down and write a paper on the strengths and weaknesses of the buying side of the company. He wrote 20 pages of elegant, densely worded reasons why various things should be done.

When he had finished, he was rather pleased with himself. He sent it to Derek Higgins.

He sat down in Derek Higgins's office and waited while the latter read carefully through it.

Derek Higgins finished reading and looked up at him. 'This is all wonderful, Jim,' he said, 'and I'm sure you're right.'

Mutter's heart soared.

'But,' Derek Higgins went on, 'at the end of the day, what I want to do is make a profit.'

Mutter returned to his office a disappointed man. But he knew he had been reminded of a simple truth. Possibly, it was a truth which Derek Higgins had not forgotten since that black day back in 1966.

'That really said it all,' Mutter recalled, 'If you make a profit, you have succeeded. In fact, many of the things I suggested in that paper were incorporated over the years. But it was a profound statement in its simplicity, and it taught me a lot.'

The Chapel of the Convent of St Vincent de Paul refurbished for the client, Sisters of
Charity of St Vincent de Paul, 1976 (Architect: Derek Arend Associates).

Mercedes Depot,
London E15, was
completed in 1991
within an extremely
tight contract time
(Architect: The
Tooley & Foster
Partnership).

Goodmayes Library, Ilford, completed 1990 (Client and Architect: London Borough of Redbridge).

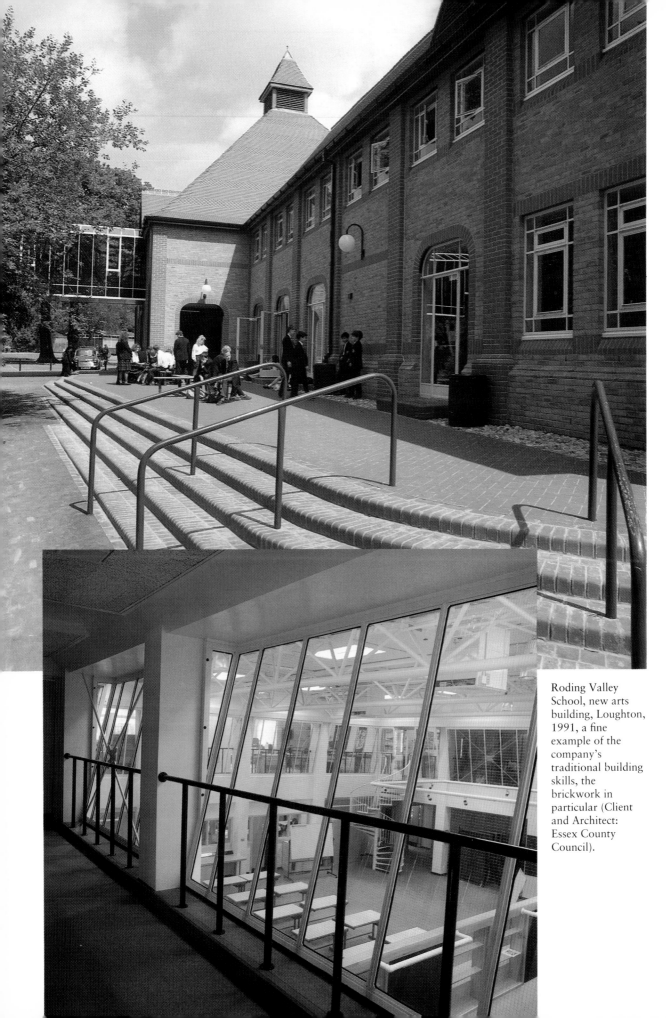

Roding Valley School, new arts building, Loughton, 1991, a fine example of the company's traditional building skills, the brickwork in particular (Client and Architect: Essex County Council).

## Chapter Three

# 21 YEARS ON

B Y the second half of the 1970s, Derek Higgins was determined that D. J. Higgins & Sons Limited should have a higher public profile. At a time when most of the building industry did not acknowledge that such a thing as marketing existed, this was an unusual move.

In March 1977, HM Queen Elizabeth the Queen Mother laid the foundation stone of the new St Saviour's Priory, rebuilt by D. J. Higgins & Sons Limited, at Haggerston Road, Dalston. The presence of royalty attracted considerable publicity.

In the autumn of the same year, the company sponsored the Vancouver Trophy sports meeting held by Woodford Green Athletic Club. The 'Woodford 800' was the star event and attracted top runners from the elite British Milers Club. George Thomas presented the first prize to Walter Wilkinson of York on behalf of D. J. Higgins & Sons Limited. The company sponsored the same meeting, and George Eastwood presented the same prize to the same winner, the following year.

Public sector contracts proceeding under the supervision of contracts managers Graham Jupp and Terry Edwards included 48 flats for Broxbourne Borough Council in Cheshunt, a children's home for Barnardos Developments in Woodford Bridge, flats for old people for

Her Majesty, Queen Elizabeth the Queen Mother, when she laid the foundation stone of the new St Saviour's Priory, London E2, in 1977, pictured here with Derek Higgins.

the Anchor Housing Association in Enfield, and alterations to Cumberland School for the London Borough of Newham.

But the building company was not only servicing the public sector. As well as the commercial and industrial sector, which was beginning to recover from the recession, clients of D. J. Higgins & Sons Limited included D. J. Higgins Developments Limited. Under contracts manager Derek Higgins himself, the company was developing new houses at Nursery Road, Loughton.

Richard Higgins had completed his training and helped run contracts for D. J. Higgins & Sons Limited at Cheshunt, Enfield and Boreham. He was becoming increasingly interested in the development business, which was run by Derek Higgins assisted by Bill Lovering. In 1978, Richard Higgins became site-based contracts manager for the development of 14 detached houses and bungalows at Sunset Avenue, Woodford Green.

In the summer of 1978, the Higgins companies were restructured into a new group. 'We needed to break the company down to make the separate parts easier to handle,' Derek Higgins commented.

D. J. Higgins Construction Limited undertook building projects above and below £1 million. D. J. Higgins Building Works Limited, run by Gordon Bent, specialised in refurbishment and rehabilitation

44-46 Mildmay Grove, Islington, refurbished for the London Borough of Islington in 1978. Local authorities increasingly practised refurbishment in the 1970s – a major opportunity which was fully grasped by Higgins.

*Left:* Chelsea Manor Buildings, Flood Walk, Chelsea, 1978 (Client: London Borough of Chelsea; Architect: Elliott & Bilton Partnership). Another refurbishment, this time on a much bigger scale.

*Below:* Tibberton Square, Islington, rehabilitation and creation of 48 new two-bedroom and one-bedroom flats for the London Borough of Islington (Architect: Andrews Sherlock & Partners) 1978. At that time one of the largest projects carried out by D. J. Higgins Building Works Limited.

work up to the value of £1 million. Gordon Bent was also Managing Director of D. J. Higgins Plant Limited. D. J. Higgins Industrial Developments Limited was established to purchase and develop industrial sites. D. J. Higgins Developments Limited continued in its existing business and D. J. Higgins & Sons Limited was the parent company.

The new group still operated from Horn Lane, but Gordon Bent was given a free hand to find premises for D. J. Higgins Building Works Ltd. This he did, and the subsidiary moved to a yard and offices at 420 High Road, Ilford, to which the plant was also moved and the old plant yards sold.

D. J. Higgins Building Works Limited became very successful at High Road, Ilford, and the upturn in refurbishment and rehabilitation activity led to a number of senior staff being transferred there from head office. One of the biggest projects undertaken by Building Works was the rehabilitation of Tibberton Square, Islington, and the creation of 48 new two-bedroom and one-bedroom flats for the London Borough of Islington. The scheme was officially opened by the Rt. Hon. Merlyn Rees MP on 10 July 1979.

D. J. Higgins Construction Limited was as energetic as ever in its pursuit of new building contracts, in the face of keen competition and a depressed climate. There were lighter moments. Princes Park Avenue,

Shepherdess Walk, London N1, completed in 1980. One of the first major refurbishment projects constructed by Higgins for a housing association (Client: Circle 33 Housing Trust Limited; Architect: Levitt Bernstein Associates).

the company's biggest contract to date, was successfully topped out after many trials and tribulations, including the issue of more than 1,500 drawings for the project. The architect marked the occasion by presenting the site agent with a Lego set.

As the Higgins Group Newsletter remarked:

Despite the ravages of the weather and the constraints of the sites, we have during the past year managed to give our clients buildings, which, in the admittedly one-sided view of all directly employed staff, are a credit to the Company, a joy to behold and a lasting monument to their initiative, resourcefulness and ability.

Derek Higgins and George Eastwood both knew the benefits of education. The company prided itself on seeing its apprentices through prosperity and recession, and it encouraged them to achieve academic success and win the certificates to prove it. In 1979, they included Richard Higgins, who, like his father before him, became a Licentiate of the Institute of Builders. David Dorrington achieved the City & Guilds qualification in Carpentry and Joinery.

Fifteen years later, Richard Higgins would be joint Chairman of Higgins Group PLC and Managing Director of D. J. Higgins Developments Limited.

In 1979, D. J. Higgins Construction Limited completed more contracts to build flats and extensions to schools for the public sector. But economic pressures on local authorities, and a greater awareness of the environmental benefits of restoring existing buildings, meant that the emphasis in the public sector was moving towards larger scale renovation projects.

An example of this was the rehabilitation of Edward Henry House behind Coin Street on the south bank of the Thames. This grim old block had originally been built to house policemen and their families by the Metropolitan Police Commissioners (who in due course had become clients of D. J. Higgins & Sons Limited). The building had undergone various modifications and stood empty for some years, before the Society of Co-Operative Dwellings secured funding to renovate it from the Greater London Council. The tender of £1.2 million was won by D. J. Higgins Building Works Limited.

In March 1979, the company started work. 'There is always something interesting in rehabilitating old buildings,' Gordon Bent remarked at the time, adding: 'The contract, despite the excellent basic structure, was not without its problems.'

These problems included the fine narrow archways which were the only access into the site, the smallness of the windows and the weakness of joists unable to support the load of new internal walls. But gradually the building was transformed. The roof became an inner city garden, balconies once used for storing coal became sources of extra space and air, and the old fireplaces serviced the new gas-fired back boiler system. The result was 66 flats for 200 people and the contract was completed in December 1981.

D. J. Higgins Construction Limited built Kestrel Court, a new sheltered housing estate in Walthamstow during this time, for Circle 33 Housing Association.

Kestrel Court and Edward Henry House proved that the housing association market could be fruitful. But it would be some time before this market was recognised as an alternative to the traditional public sector, and the important source of clients that it represents today.

Stephen Higgins joined D. J. Higgins & Sons Limited in 1981 and became involved in the marketing side of the business. Martin Higgins, the youngest of the three sons, joined D. J. Higgins Developments Limited in 1981 after working for Ambrose, a leading local estate agent. He was responsible for properties built by the development company through the design stage to sale. Ten years later, Stephen and Martin Higgins would be appointed to join Richard and Derek Higgins and others on the board of the new parent company, Higgins Group PLC.

Also in 1981, Benny King joined D. J. Higgins & Sons Limited as a contracts manager. Benny King progressed through the roles of senior contracts manager and contracts director, and became Managing Director of D. J. Higgins & Sons Limited in 1989.

In 1981, D. J. Higgins & Sons Limited was still the parent company, the board being chaired by Derek Higgins, and the directors including George Eastwood. Richard Higgins too became a director and the following year was joined on the board by Gordon Bent and Barry Penman.

1982 was the group's twenty-first year in business. D. J. Higgins & Sons Limited and its subsidiary companies had a workforce of 300 and 26 apprentices in training. Half of these were carpenters, seven were plumbers and four were bricklayers. The company also had trainee surveyors and estimators who would eventually become managers. Of the apprentices, many would stay, some would leave, and some would return.

The Higgins Group had a turnover of £14 million and 26 current contracts, 60 per cent of which were new building projects. The Group had a new motto, 'Building a Greater London', which summed up the basis of its current success.

But Derek Higgins was thinking ahead. 'It is not enough to be a good builder,' he said, 'we have to sell ourselves. 'The time has come, too, when we must move into the private sector, because there is not nearly enough local authority work, once the bread and butter of the company.'

The Higgins Group celebrated its twenty-first anniversary with a dinner and dance at the Savoy Hotel, London, on 6 March 1982. The 400 guests included many staff, clients and suppliers.

George Eastwood led the toast to the guests. The response was led by a friend from the earliest days, George Coppen, former chief buyer of W. & C. French.

Dick White, of the architects White and Mileson, toasted D. J.

Derek Higgins (centre), George Eastwood, wives and colleagues celebrated the company's twenty-first birthday at the Savoy, 6 March 1982 (from *Guardian & Gazette*).

Higgins & Sons Limited. This was to have been proposed by Col. Sir Arthur Noble, former employer of Derek Higgins and George Eastwood at W. & C. French. Sir Arthur, who had taken great pleasure in their progress since then, had died suddenly the week before.

Derek Higgins responded on behalf of the Group: 'I have been given strict instructions to resist the temptation to wallow in nostalgia this evening,' he said, 'but such is the occasion that I am sure most of you would like me to tell you very briefly about the origins of the company.'

He paid tribute to George Eastwood, and his father-in-law Bill Pardey, who was 88: 'he's still going strong – he is with us here tonight – we couldn't keep him away.'

He paid tribute to the staff and the team spirit within the Group. 'We are a family company; these days one tends to hear less about the individual and so much more about the State and what the State can do for us, but in my opinion in the end we are dealing with people as individuals – and it is having the ability to recognise this and being able to communicate with people at all different levels which is one reason why we have succeeded.

'One definition of the word 'Family' that I discovered, was 'a body of employees or volunteer workers united in a common enterprise'. That, ladies and gentlemen, is D. J. Higgins & Sons Limited.'

He also paid tribute to his wife Olive, and to Gladys Smith, his secretary of almost 20 years: 'Gladys Smith has been a model of loyalty and integrity,' he told the assembled guests, 'and we all wish her a speedy recovery from her recent illness.'

Her friends and colleagues knew Gladys Smith was desperately ill. But she was determined to attend the Savoy celebrations. Derek Higgins was acknowledging her spirit.

Gladys Smith died less than a month after the twenty-first anniversary celebrations of the company of which she had been a such a loyal part. On the morning of her funeral, Derek Higgins conducted a brief service in her memory in the yard at Horn Lane.

# Chapter Four

# BUILDING A GREATER LONDON

IN 1983, George Eastwood, who was five years older than Derek Higgins, retired at the age of 59 from the board of the business he had helped found 22 years earlier. The directors and longstanding professional associates met at Derek Higgins's home to honour him.

As Derek Higgins would recall: 'The company was built on the strength of the association of George Eastwood and myself; with Olive's wholehearted support. George and I could always see the funny side of things. We could always make the best of it – and we were often working until 10 o'clock at night.'

Of his long career and many adventures with Derek Higgins, Eastwood would say: 'Derek and I had great harmony. He used to be ill every year with bronchitis and I was left running the firm. Then he would recover and I would become ill instead.

'We learned a lot, and grew up, in a way that would not have happened otherwise.'

George Eastwood would remain on close terms with Derek Higgins. The three Higgins sons would always regard him as part of the family.

Of his five children, his son Steven Eastwood qualified as a surveyor. Steven Eastwood took charge of D. J. Higgins & Sons Limited's growing computer systems, a role in which he would still be flourishing ten years later.

That same year, D. J. Higgins & Sons Limited apprentices swept the board at the National Federation of Building Trades Employers annual awards for the London Region, winning 14 prizes. The company still prided itself that its apprentices were part of the accumulated skills and experience of its direct labour force.

Also in 1983, Alan Moran joined D. J. Higgins & Sons Limited as senior estimator. Moran progressed through the roles of chief estimator and estimating director, and joined the board of D. J. Higgins & Sons Limited in 1990.

D. J. Higgins Construction Limited was completing Phase One of a new building project in Albion Drive, Shrubland Road and Brownlow Road, Dalston, for the London Borough of Hackney. This was a public sector contract of 12 seven-person houses and 24 two-person flats in a modern classical style.

D. J. Higgins Building Works Limited was also active in nearby Hackney. Lennox House in Cresset Road, Hackney, was built in 1937 by the Bethnal Green & East London Housing Association to ease appalling slum conditions in the East End. Nearly 50 years later, the same housing association employed D. J. Higgins Building Works Limited to refurbish and rehabilitate this large scheme providing accommodation for 93 people.

Lennox House was officially opened by HRH the Duke of Kent on 10 July 1984. During his tour of the buildings, an elderly resident showed the Duke a photograph of his father opening the original flats in 1937.

In 1985, Bill Pardey, Derek Higgins's father-in-law and the first employee of D. J. Higgins & Sons Limited, died at the age of 91, having joined the company at an age by which most men have retired.

The construction and rehabilitation companies carried out these and many other sizeable contracts during the early 1980s. D. J. Higgins Construction Limited won public sector contracts worth many millions of pounds and built flats, houses and health centres in Dalston, Walthamstow, Edmonton, Finchley and Crouch Hill.

D. J. Higgins Building Works Limited won similar-sized public sector contracts to rehabilitate flats and houses in Hackney, Hammersmith, Earls Court, Islington and Stepney. This was a far cry from the days when Derek and Olive Higgins could drive around all the sites in the course of a single day.

The Higgins Group of Companies was living up to its motto of 'Building a Greater London.' But, although turnover was healthy, costs in the capital had continued to rise and erode those narrow profit margins.

The official opening in 1984, by HRH the Duke of Kent, of Lennox House, Cresset Road, London E9 (Client: Bethel Green & East London Housing Association; Architect: MEPK Architects).

The annual prizegiving of the Building Employer Confederation, 1988, at which prizes were awarded to 15 Higgins Group apprentices, beating Higgins' own record of 14 apprentices in 1983. Derek Higgins (standing centre) with colleagues and prizewinners (from *Guardian & Gazette*).

As Derek Higgins had foreseen, the local authority work which had transformed the company from a domestic jobbing builder into a major public sector contractor, was no longer enough. The construction company had also carried out commercial and industrial contracts for British Aerospace Pension Fund Trustees in Acton, Trustee Savings Bank in Blackfriars, Midland Bank in Enfield and Bejam Freezer Food Centres in Hertford. Contracts for Norwich Union Life Assurance Group in Fitzrovia, Crusader Insurance in Covent Garden and Pearl Assurance in the West End were also under way. The Higgins Group had to penetrate further into the private sector if it was going to build a greater future for itself, too.

The Ilford headquarters of D. J. Higgins Building Works Limited was closed down and the company returned to Horn Lane, where the parent company had already acquired the houses opposite and next door.

Gordon Bent, who managed the rehabilitation and refurbishment company, applied his talents to generating business. Bent was a motivator of staff and an energetic marketing man with a wealth of contacts going back many years which he cultivated assiduously in the interests of the company.

With the help of Steven Eastwood, Bent also purchased a powerful computer and devised the company's first computerised marketing

Higgins Group PLC Board 1990.
Left to right: Robert Horvath,
Gordon Bent, Derek Higgins,
Richard Higgins and Olive Higgins.

programme. This was the forerunner of the sophisticated systems maintained and updated on a regular basis by the Business Development Department of the company today.

The run of public sector contracts continued through the early and middle 1980s, and the growth of the private commercial sector gave the first hints of the boom years to come. The company built a new health centre in Walthamstow and new flats and houses in East Ham, and refurbished flats in Bermondsey, Islington, Hackney and Stepney.

In the private sector it carried out new building contracts for Investors in Industry Developments Limited in Waltham Cross, Bejam Freezer Food Centres in Walthamstow, Arlington Motor Company PLC in Ponders End, Cobden Developments Limited in Bromley and Look Ahead (Beacon Hostels) Housing Association Limited in Bethnal Green.

New members of the company included Brian Hamilton, who joined D. J. Higgins & Sons Limited in 1986 as Surveying Director. Hamilton would be appointed to the board of D. J. Higgins & Sons Limited in 1989.

Among the private sector clients in 1987 was D. J. Higgins & Sons Limited; the company was building itself a new headquarters.

No. 173 Horn Lane and its satellites were filled to capacity. What had started life as a family house with a yard and small office at the rear, had become a sprawling operation with difficult access.

Hawke House, the new headquarters of D. J. Higgins & Sons, was under construction by the company at Old Station Road, Loughton. The site had previously been occupied by a garage and spotted as suitable for development by Martin Higgins, who had worked for the estate agent next door. The new headquarters was named after one of the houses at Loughton School, which Derek, Richard and Martin Higgins had attended.

Hawke House was topped out on 2 June 1987, by Councillor Reg Amanet, Chairman of Epping Forest District Council. The £750,000, three-storey building was designed by architects White & Mileson and had 10,500 square feet of modern office space, a high speed lift, full central heating, under-floor communication trunking and parking for 33 cars.

Richard Higgins presented Mr Amanet with a cheque for the Fire Service Benevolent Fund. He said the family had a sentimental attachment to Horn Lane. 'We started the business there,' he said, 'and turned over £9,705 9s. 0d. in 1961. Now we have 50 sites and our turnover is between £20 and £25 million.'

Derek Higgins commented on the proximity of the fire station. 'Later this year, we will become the Fire Service's new neighbours,' he said, 'Although we don't envisage using their services in the foreseeable future, we hope our small donation can be put to good use.'

D. J. Higgins & Sons Limited moved into Hawke House early in November 1987. Derek Higgins, leaning out of a second-storey window, took possession of a giant key from Richard Higgins, perched on the end of a 100 foot turntable ladder extended courtesy of the local fire brigade.

At first, even Derek Higgins wondered if the new building was too big, and that they might have to let part of it. He invited an old school friend, Canon Jeffrey Holley of St John's Church in Loughton, to come and bless it.

The staff attended and there was tea and cakes. Canon Holley duly performed the ceremony. 'Oh, Lord,' he said, 'Please make sure they make a profit.'

Within a short time, they found they did not have to let part of the building after all.

No. 173 Horn Lane was demolished. The company built and sold a block of flats on the site.

'We should have moved years earlier,' Derek Higgins recalled, 'It held back the business. My sons made me realise; and since we moved, the business has taken off.'

Olive Higgins did not watch the demolition. 'I'm not a person to go back,' she recalled, 'it seems such a long while ago, now. When you think back, things were quite hard, really. But I knew we would be all right.'

Richard Higgins watched the demolition. A piece of old wallpaper that was suddenly exposed triggered memories of his childhood and the years spent working at that address. Building was part of the fabric of the Higgins family. Now, like the family, the business had truly come of age.

Cumberland Court, Horn Lane, the block of eight flats which replaced the original office (Client: D. J. Higgins Developments Limited).

In the last six months of 1987, D. J. Higgins & Sons Limited and its associated companies had won contracts worth £14 million.

The London Borough of Lewisham awarded a £4 million contract to build a two-storey housing scheme in Honor Oak. The London Borough of Islington awarded a £4 million contract to build 70 flats and maisonettes. Anglia Secure Homes awarded a £1.3 million contract to build 46 retirement flats in Wanstead. Other contracts included a business centre industrial development for Land and Urban PLC, and homes for the elderly in Chigwell for the Leonard Cheshire Foundation.

The group had a new headquarters, 220 full-time staff and an annual turnover of £30 million:

'Last year was a good one,' Derek Higgins remarked. But his mind would soon be less on how the business had flourished during the boom, as on how it would flourish in future. For the collapse of the stock markets in October 1987 signalled that the latest cycle of boom years was coming to an end, as they had done before, and always do.

# Chapter Five

# HIGGINS GROUP PLC

THE late 1980s saw the Higgins Group of Companies grow very substantially in both its construction and development activities, to the point where its turnover had more than doubled since the beginning of the decade.

In 1988, the construction business followed its record year of 1987 with a stream of contracts in the public, commercial and industrial sectors. D. J. Higgins & Sons Limited won contracts to build and refurbish flats in Islington, Tooting, Chelmsford and Southwark. Higgins's apprentices beat their 1983 record by winning 15 prizes at the National Federation of Building Trades Employers Awards. Higgins was one of 24 firms out of 130 who entered to win a gold medal in the Considerate Contractor Awards, given by the City of London Corporation to contractors who maintained a high quality of management and orderliness at their sites in the City. Don Price retired as Estimating Director, after 17 years with the Group.

The development business grew with the times, after the uncertainties of the 1960s and the turbulence of the 1970s. The easy availability of bank lending and the booming economic climate, meant that both the developer and customer found the idea of high-quality newly built housing a more attractive proposition than ever. D. J. Higgins Developments Limited, with Richard Higgins as Managing Director, Stephen Higgins as Company Secretary and Martin Higgins as Sales Director, built a £2.3 million group of 48 sheltered-housing flats at Chadwell Heath and 19 flats at Stratford, as well as the Sally Lunn development of eleven detached houses at Ongar and others.

But, it is a fact of life in the building industry that the construction and development businesses are contra-cyclical. When one does well, the other may do less well. The reasons have little to do with the calibre of the management and staff of the individual construction and development company.

In the late 1980s, the banks were willing to lend any amount of money to developers. Clients were buying new-build flats and houses on the strength of a set of plans alone. The construction industry, on the other hand, suffered in this kind of climate.

Subcontractors walked out, in pursuit of quicker money elsewhere. Costs rose rapidly and once again threatened tight schedules and narrow profit margins.

D. J. Higgins Developments Limited and D. J. Higgins & Sons Limited were no exception to these pressures. But the growth of the development business, and the fact that the construction business was

The presentation in 1984 by Derek Higgins of his company's gift of a portable utility and storage unit at the Jubilee Lodge Centre, Chigwell, through the charity, Winged Fellowship, which provides holidays for physically disabled people. Ten years later Derek Higgins was appointed Chairman of the Winged Fellowship Eastern Region Appeal.

weathering these pressures, meant that the Higgins Group as a whole made an attractive proposition to a cash-rich developer looking to acquire an established building company.

In the late 1980s, an approach of precisely this kind was made by a potential buyer. It was politely rejected. As Derek Higgins had said of 1972: 'It's never wrong to sell'; but that had been in the context of a new development, and in a falling rather than a rising market.

The increasing profitability of the Group prompted the management to examine ways of growing further and capitalising on the current climate. They came to the conclusion that the best way to achieve this was to convert the existing companies into a public limited company, with a view to seeking flotation on the London Stock Exchange. Throughout late 1988 and early 1989, they laid the foundations of Higgins Group PLC.

The company became a public limited company – Higgins Group PLC – in February 1989. The first directors were Derek Higgins and Richard Higgins. They were joined in August 1989 by Olive Higgins, who resigned from the board in December 1990, Gordon Bent, who resigned from the board and retired from the company in February 1992, and Robert Horvath, who arrived after 12 years with Price Waterhouse. The present board consists of Derek Higgins (Joint

Chairman), Richard Higgins (Joint Chairman), Stephen Higgins, Martin Higgins and Robert Horvath as Finance Director.

Higgins Group PLC consists of four companies, D. J. Higgins & Sons Limited, D. J. Higgins Developments Limited, D. J. Higgins Investments Limited and D. J. Higgins City Limited.

D. J. Higgins & Sons Limited refurbishes, builds and designs for clients in the public and private sectors. The present board consists of Derek Higgins (Joint Chairman), Richard Higgins (Joint Chairman), Stephen Higgins, Robert Horvath (Company Secretary), Benny King (Managing Director), Bryan Sabin, Brian Hamilton, Jim Mutter and Alan Moran.

D. J. Higgins Developments Limited undertakes residential, commercial and industrial developments. The present board consists of Derek Higgins (Joint Chairman), Richard Higgins (Joint Chairman and Managing Director), Stephen Higgins (Company Secretary), Martin Higgins and Robert Horvath.

D. J. Higgins Investments Limited covers a range of residential, commercial and industrial developments. The present board consists of Derek Higgins (Joint Chairman), Richard Higgins (Joint Chairman), Stephen Higgins (Company Secretary), Martin Higgins and Robert Horvath.

D. J. Higgins City Limited, formed in October 1993, undertakes new building and refurbishment in the City and West End of London. The present board consists of Stephen Higgins (Chairman), Jeff Rawlins (Managing Director), Robert Horvath, Benny King and Bryan Sabin.

Higgins Group PLC was incorporated at a time when the development business was booming and the construction business was holding its own in spite of inflating costs and fickle labour. The restructuring of the Group, and the combination of experience and new blood on the boards of the companies, enabled these costs to be addressed effectively and meant that the contracting business continued to grow.

Higgins Group PLC won contracts worth £7.8 million in the first four months of 1989. These included refurbishment works for the London Borough of Southwark, and the Property Services Agency at Basildon; new school building for Essex County Council; and contracts for D. J. Higgins Developments Limited to build an industrial complex at Epping and houses at Loughton.

But, although there was a time lag between the two events, the collapse of the stock market in late 1987 slowly began to make itself felt on builders and developers. Once again, the contra-cyclical relationship between the two became clear; only this time, while the contracting business recovered control of its costs and there were fewer labour problems, the development business began to shiver in the cooling climate.

D. J. Higgins Developments Limited successfully brought its developments of 62 retirement flats at Limewood Court, Gants Hill, onto

Bouverie Road, London N16. The
success of this scheme led to the
negotiation of a further phase for
the construction of special needs
building for the elderly and infirm
(Client: New Islington & Hackney
Housing Association; Architect:
Anthony Richardson & Partners).

the market, and 48 retirement flats at Chadwell Heath would follow.
The development company projected healthy profits for 1990 and
1991; but the recession meant that, in the event, the company broke
even that year and recorded a loss the year after.

As Robert Horvath said: 'We simply liquidated our stock. Derek
Higgins had done it at least twice before, and this was no different.'

'We probably came out even,' Richard Higgins recalled, 'whereas a
lot of contractors with a bit of spare money drifted into development
for all the wrong reasons. Now we have a number of sites, we haven't
paid too much for the land, we have joint ventures, we presell, and we
market ourselves effectively. So things look good.'

The consolidation of the construction business, and the effects of the
recession on developments, meant that, unlike some newly incorporated
public companies who later regretted it, Higgins Group PLC resisted
the temptation to plunge headlong into flotation on the Stock
Exchange. Instead, it concentrated on marketing itself more aggressively
in new areas of development and construction, and building on its
established expertise.

In 1990, Bryan Sabin joined the board of D. J. Higgins & Sons
Limited as Business Development Director. Sabin was a qualified
quantity surveyor, and his experience as a building industry professional
commended him to Derek Higgins, who had himself spent many years
marketing the company.

As Derek Higgins had predicted, local authorities could no longer be
expected to supply sufficient contracts in the short term. Tenders had
dropped in size and frequency, government cut-backs had bitten deeper,

building administration departments of local council were being slashed to the bone. Old contacts were disappearing and few new ones were taking their place.

'The 1980s were about niches,' said Sabin, 'You found one, you got in there and you dominated it. In the 1990s, a lot of those companies have fallen away because they were not flexible enough to change.

'So, we hit upon this community spectrum: housing (new-build social housing and urban regeneration in terms of refurbishment), health and education. We pointed the company in establishing itself as what we called a community contractor.'

This was an idea Derek Higgins had been exploring since the early 1980s. A report compiled by Sabin identified this and many more areas where Higgins Group PLC had begun to build up data on which to base its strategy.

Many of the predictions in the report proved to be correct. One area which the report had underestimated, however, was just how steep and fast the descent into recession would be. Had the board of D. J. Higgins & Sons Limited, and Derek Higgins in particular, not placed their full weight behind the recommendations, it might have been a different story.

D. J. Higgins & Sons Limited was awarded major contracts in 1990 to build houses and flats in Newham, to repair an estate in Hackney, to improve a block of flats for the City of Westminster and to carry out other work in Tower Hamlets.

Pickfords Wharf, the first part of the 70 home development built by D. J. Higgins & Sons Limited for Islington Council, was officially opened by the Rt. Hon. Bryan Gould MP on 24 April 1990. In June 1990, Derek Higgins and snooker and boxing impresario Barry Hearn

Pickford's Wharf, London N1, a 70-home development was officially opened by Rt Hon Bryan Gould in April 1990. Since the completion of this project in 1990 Islington Council have carried out no further significant new-build housing schemes (Client: London Borough of Islington; Architect: London Borough of Islington).

Wellington Avenue
School, Chingford,
completed 1992
(Client and
Architect: London
Borough of
Waltham Forest).

*Right:* Westminster Court, Wanstead, a sheltered housing scheme, 1988 (Client: Anglia Secure Homes PLC).

*Below:* Bethnal Green Estate, Tower Hamlets, London. A major 'tenants in occupation' project involving considerable tenant liaison skills. Seven blocks comprising 122 dwellings were fully refurbished, 1991 (Client: London Borough of Tower Hamlets; Architect: Pearlman Moiret Associates).

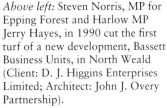

*Above left:* Steven Norris, MP for Epping Forest and Harlow MP Jerry Hayes, in 1990 cut the first turf of a new development, Bassett Business Units, in North Weald (Client: D. J. Higgins Enterprises Limited; Architect: John J. Overy Partnership).

*Above right:* Official opening of Bassett Business Units by Baroness Denton accompanied by Councillor Anne Miller, the Rt Hon Steven Norris MP and Derek Higgins.

of Matchroom Limited laid the final floor panel at the topping out ceremony of the four-storey, 21,000-square foot office block developed and built by the company at South Street, Romford, later to be occupied by Polygram UK Limited. In September 1990, Lord Young, Alan Sugar, Derek Higgins and Lord Sieff opened the Nathan Sugar and Rita Simons Special Care Wing at Vi & John Rubens House, Ilford, built by D. J. Higgins & Sons Limited.

In the autumn of 1990, Harlow MP Jerry Hayes and Epping Forest MP Steven Norris cut the first turf on the site of a joint venture between Higgins Group PLC, Epping Forest District Council and Forest Enterprise Agency Trust. Bassett Business Units Limited was a development of 25 units for small businesses at a site on North Weald Aerodrome in Essex. The aim was to help small businesses to grow and flourish by providing a complete package of services in an attractive custom-built environment, a commitment that was inspired by the growth of D. J. Higgins & Sons Limited from a small business into Higgins Group PLC.

Higgins Group PLC announced that it had won contracts worth £3 million to build 22 houses at Upton Park for the East London Housing Association, and refurbish Wharfedale Court, 36 flats in Gilpin Square, for the London Borough of Hackney. Both these contracts were on a design-and-build basis, where the contractor took responsibility for the design.

This had not traditionally been a favoured way for D. J. Higgins &
Sons to carry out contracts. But the change signalled the company's
move into tendering aggressively for contracts in a new market, where
cost controls could make this approach feasible; a market it had hither-
to hardly explored. Today, 'design and build' accounts for 30 per cent
of D. J. Higgins & Sons' overall business.

In 1991, as the recession deepened, architects, surveyors and builders
all shed jobs simply to survive. Large-scale local authority projects
were few and far between. A survey showed that, in 1990, 56 per cent
of all new architectural commissions in London were either cancelled
or postponed. Between 1990 and 1991, the proportion of local authority projects in the overall workload of D. J. Higgins & Sons Limited
had fallen from 83 to 44 per cent.

Yet, D. J. Higgins & Sons Limited had not only managed to main-
tain its market share in certain areas, but also found new ones in this
depressed climate.

Alan Sugar with Derek Higgins at
the opening of the Nathan Sugar
and Rita Simons special care wing
at Vi & John Rubens House. Ilford
(Client: Jewish Welfare Board;
Architect: Sidney Kaye Firmin).

Emmanuel Church Billericay, completed 1992 (Client: Parochial Church Council of Billericay; Architect MEB Partnership).

*Opposite page:* Cann Hall Methodist Church, Leytonstone, 1992 (Employer: Managing Trustees of Cann Hall Methodist Church; Employer's Agent: E.C. Harris; Architect: Pearlman Moiret Associates).

Ron Hatch on his retirement after 25 years with the Higgins Group, flanked by (from left to right) Martin, Richard, Derek, Olive and Stephen Higgins.

One reason for this was the fact that the company was now on the approved lists of 41 housing associations, a move that would leave other builders up to a year behind. By the time other companies realised the potential of this market, D. J. Higgins & Sons Limited would have established itself as a leader in this field.

Angell Town, Brixton, was another landmark scheme for D. J. Higgins & Sons Limited at this time. The contract with London Borough of Lambeth was to regenerate an inner city estate in an area notorious for low living standards and high levels of crime and unemployment. The company was asked what else it could do for the community in return.

Eighteen youngsters from the estate were enrolled on an estate-based apprenticeship scheme, started and funded by D. J. Higgins & Sons Limited. The scheme provided a proper apprenticeship in various trades, with site experience and college release. It has since been recognised as an essential part of estate-regeneration planning.

Also in 1991, Higgins apprentices won 13 awards at the annual prize-giving of the National Federation of Building Trades Employers.

But, whether it was on the estates or through the more conventional route, to Derek Higgins the importance of giving greater opportunities to young people remained. 'We've had apprentices for a long time, but it's harder now to take on the number that we did. Most builders sublet, and there aren't the government grants there used to be. We don't have enough permanent tradesmen to put them all with.'

Higgins Group PLC was as active as ever in sponsoring youth teams in hockey, cricket and football. Derek Higgins believes that sport is good for young people. 'It uses their energy, gives them team spirit and a respect for discipline. We believe in it. We promote it the whole time. There are a million people unemployed in this country under the age of 25. It's a terrible waste.'

The success of Angell Town, and the establishment of the estate apprenticeship scheme. not only helped the local environment but gave D. J. Higgins & Sons Limited a higher profile at the Department of the Environment.

Since the early 1990s, Higgins Group PLC has undertaken many joint developments with housing associations and estate-regeneration contracts for the public sector.

Wellington Avenue, Chingford, is a joint venture between D. J. Higgins Developments Limited, Circle 33 Housing Trust, John Grooms Housing Association and Circle 33 Home Ownership, for 100 homes for rent and 18 for shared-equity sale.

Elmcroft Avenue, Wanstead, is a joint venture between D. J. Higgins Developments Limited and Circle 33 Housing Trust of 53 homes for rent and 30 homes for private sale by the company.

D. J. Higgins & Sons Limited, in conjunction with Circle 33

Derek Higgins is an enthusiast of sport. Here he is seen as team Captain with rival Captain, Peter Edmonson, Chairman of Anglia Secure Homes PLC, together with internationals John Childs and John Lever, on the occasion of a charity cricket match at Frinton-on-Sea in 1988.

Greencroft Gardens, Hampstead. Refurbishment of this residential building was completed in 1992 (Client: Fairhazel Co-Operative Limited; Architect: Levitt Bernstein Associates).

*Left:* Wellington Avenue, Chingford, completed in 1992. One of Higgins's biggest developments to date, it was the successful outcome of a significant partnership between housing associations and developer. It was featured in Building Together, published by the National Federation of Housing Associations (Clients: Higgins Group PLC and Circle 33 Housing Trust Limited; Architect: Phippen Randall & Parkes).

*Below:* Angell Town, Brixton, completed in 1993. A landmark for the company in which it established a strong relationship with the residents, including an estate-based apprenticeship scheme and the sponsorship of a children's theatre production (Clients: London Borough of Lambeth and Angell Town Community; Architects: Burrell Foley Fisher).

The Higgins Group PLC Board.
Left to right: Robert Horvath,
Martin, Richard, Stephen and
(seated) Derek Higgins.

Housing Trust and the local authority, has designed and built 100 units
for rent and 18 for shared ownership by the local community; the £7
million scheme also includes dwellings designed specifically for the disabled. As well as Angell Town, the company has also won contracts to
refurbish estates in the Harrow Road, Notting Hill and at Gloucester
Grove, near North Peckham.

'Absolutely brilliant,' was how the
secretary of the tenants' association
described the refurbishment, in
1992, of Wharfedale Court in
Hackney. She is shown here with
Roger Wilson of D. J. Higgins &
Sons Limited and the Leader of the
Council. This design and build
contract was, unusually and very
successfully, carried out while the
occupiers were in residence (Client
and Architect: London Borough of
Hackney).

Higgins Group PLC is actively involved in the community. Derek Higgins, formerly a keen hockey player, here receives an award from the Sports Council on behalf of the Old Loughtonians Hockey Club (whose clubhouse was built by the company in 1978).

In 1992, Higgins Group PLC, with Derek Higgins and his three sons on the board, turned over £38 million and recorded pre-tax profits of £0.5 million; a respectable result in the current climate.

Today, tenders by Higgins Group PLC to the private and public sectors involve millions of pounds. These contracts help to improve the environment in which we live. Higgins Group PLC and its four companies has a combined turnover of nearly £60 million. It is an established builder and developer, with the expertise and the capability to compete successfully in the public, private, commercial and industrial markets.

The issue of flotation is an option for the company. Derek Higgins is approaching his fiftieth year in the industry. Flotation would be the culmination of a lifetime's achievement. But, after a lifetime building a business, the climate for the entrance of institutional shareholders has to be right. Regardless of Derek Higgins's retirement, and of whether or not flotation takes place, Higgins Group PLC will continue to grow, because it has strong market support and a clear-minded and determined strategy.

D. J. Higgins & Sons Limited was built on the support of Olive Higgins for her husband, and the clear-mindedness and determination of Derek Higgins and George Eastwood. D. J. Higgins & Sons Limited grew with the help of Gordon Bent and many others into the D. J. Higgins Group of Companies. The D. J. Higgins Group of Companies has grown through the team effort of family and staff at all levels, into the mature organisation of today.

Today, success in the construction and development industry requires the ability to balance many qualities: leadership and team-work, aggression and flexibility, vision and the ability to change with a changing climate. This kind of success requires management and individualism, and an organisation that knows the virtues of allowing one to exist with the other. This is the kind of virtue that comes with experience, rather than innocence. The boom of the late 1980s, and recession of the early 1990s, were just two extreme examples of that changing climate. The qualities on which Higgins Group PLC was built, have taken it through those extremes, and will see Higgins Group PLC flourish in the climate of the 1990s and beyond.

Hazelbourne Nursing Home, London SW12, completed 1993 (Client: West Lambeth Health Authority; Architect: Greenhill Jenner Partnership).

*Opposite page above:* Farrier Street, London NW1, completed 1993, was opened by Marion Franks of the Housing Corporation (Client and Architect: Ujima Housing Association).

*Opposite page below:* The Fountain, Westwood Hill, London SE26, 1993, a hospice for people with AIDS or HIV positive, to be managed by the Phoenix Trust (Client: London & Quadrant Housing Trust; Architect: Levitt Bernstein Associates).

# INDEX

Note: Page numbers in **bold** type indicate illustrations; numbers in *italicised bold* type denote text and illustration on the same page.

Acton 42
Amanet, Reg 43
Andrews Sherlock & Partners **35**
Anglia Secure Homes PLC 44, 51, 57
Anthony Richardson & Partners 48
Arlington Motor Company PLC 43
Attwater & Lyle 8

Barnardos Developments 33
Barnet 24
Basildon 13, 47
Bassett Business Units *52*
Bejam Freezer Food Centres 42, 43
Bent, Gordon 16, 26, 34, 37, *42*, 63;
  becomes director of parent company 38;
  devises first computerised marketing
  programme 42-3; given free hand to
  find premises for Building Works 36;
  retirement from company 46
Bent (H.) & Co. 16
Bermondsey 43
Bethnal Green 43, **51**
Bethnal Green & East London Housing
  Association *41*
Billericay **54**
Birch, Gerald 8, 13
Black Monday 14
Blackfriars 42
B'Nai Brith Housing Association 28
Boreham 34
British Aerospace Pension Fund Trustees
  42
British Milers Club 33
Brixton, Angell Town 56, 57, 59, 60
Bromley 43
Broxbourne Borough Council 33
Buckhurst Hill 7, 8, 15, 16, 24; Higgins
  family home, Roebuck Lane 9; Roding
  Lane 10; Stag Lane 25
Building Employers Confederation 41
Bull, Michael 8
Burrell Foley Fisher **59**

Canvey Island 15, 17, 23, 24
Carr Goldsmith & Fallek **21**
Chadwell Heath 45, 48
Chelmsford 45
Chelsea Manor Buildings **35**
Cheshunt 33, 34
Chigwell 25, 44, **46**
Childs, John 57
Chingford 26, 50, 57, 59
Circle 33: Home Ownership 57; Housing
  Association 38; Housing Trust Limited
  **36**, 57, 59, 60
City and Guilds 37
City of London 20, 45, 47
City of Westminster 49
Cobden Developments Limited 43
Coe, Arthur 26
Collins, Tony 17, 25
Convent of St Vincent de Paul 29
Coppen, George 38
Crouch Hill 41
Crusader Insurance 42
Cyprus 8

*Daily Mirror* 8
Dalston *33*, 40, 41
Davies, Bill 8
Denton, Baroness **52**
Department of the Environment 57
Derek Arend Associates **29**
Dorrington, David 37
Earls Court 41
East Barnet District Urban District
  Council 13
East Ham 43
East London Housing Association 52
Eastwood, George 9, 11-14 *passim*, 24,
  25, 33; and benefits of education 37;
  company's twenty-first anniversary 38,
  **39**; clearmindedness and determination
  63; sporting activities 15, 26, 27;
  retiral 40; startup with Derek 7, 8, 10
Eastwood, Steven 40, 42
Edmonson, Peter 57
Edmonton 41
Edwards, Terry 26, 33
Enfield 34, 42
Epping 47
Epping Forest District Council 43, *52*
Essex County Council 10, 13, 17, 23, 26,
  32, 47

Fairhazel Co-Operative Limited 58
Finchley 41
Fire Service Benevolent Fund 43
Fitzrovia 42
Ford van 9

Forest Enterprise Agency Trust 52
Forest Gate 13
Foster (Charles S.) & Sons 7
Franks, Marion **61**
French Kier 8
French (W. & C.) **8**, 9, 11, 24, 38, 39
Frinton-on-Sea 57
Fyfield 13

Gants Hill 47
Gee Walker & Slater Limited 8
Golders Green 28
Gould, Bryan **49**
Greater London 7, 23; Council 37
Green Lloyd 20
Greenhill Jenner Partnership **63**
*Guardian and Gazette* 39, 41

Hackney 24, 40, *41*, 43, 49, **60**; contracts
  worth £3 million 52
Hamilton, Brian 8, 43, 47
Hammersmith 41
Hampstead, Greencroft Gardens 58
Harlow 23, 52
Harris, E. C. 55
Hatch, Ron 13, 17, **56**
Havering **18**, 23, 27
Hawke House 2, 43, 44
Hawkwell 24
Hayes, Jerry 33
Health and Safety at Work Act (1974)
  26
Hertford 42
Hertfordshire 7, 23
Higgins, Bob (brother of Derek) 7, 10
Higgins, Derek *9*, 10-14 *passim*, 28, 34;
  ambitious to extend Developments
  24-5; background and marriage 7;
  Bassett Business Units opening **52**;
  Building Employers Confederation
  prizegiving **41**; clearmindedness and
  determination 63; community
  contractor idea 49; company's first
  lorry 13; company's twenty-first
  birthday 38, **39**; dismay at bank
  manager 8; education 7, 37; first
  Director of Higgins Group PLC 46;
  Group Board **42**, 60, 61; letter
  appointing to first job 7; local
  authority work no longer enough 40,
  42, 48; Nathan Sugar and Rita
  Simons Special Care Wing, Ilford,
  opening **52**, 53; pay slip (1960) 8;
  presentation at Jubilee Lodge Centre,
  Chigwell **46**; recession and stock
  liquidation 48; Ron Hatch's retirement
  **56**; sporting activities 15, 26-7, 56,
  **57**, **61**; takes possession of key to
  Hawke House 44; with the Queen
  Mother 33
Higgins (D. J.) Building Works Limited
  34, **35**, 37, 40-1, 42
Higgins (D. J.) City Limited 36
Higgins (D. J.) Construction Limited 34,
  36, 37, 38, 41; growing computer
  systems 40
Higgins (D. J.) Developments Limited
  25, 33, 36-8 *passim*, 44, 47, 57; first
  sheltered housing scheme **21**; incorporated (1965) 13; Richard appointed
  Managing Director 45; turnover 28
Higgins (D. J.) Enterprises Limited 52
Higgins Group PLC **22**, 37, 45-63;
  actively involved in the community
  **61**; Board (1990) **42**; computer
  systems 42-3; profits 61; turnover 7,
  61
Higgins (D. J.) Industrial Developments
  Limited 36
Higgins (D. J.) Investments Limited 36
Higgins (D. J.) Plant Limited 36
Higgins (D. J.) & Sons Limited 8, 17,
  34, 36, 47, **60**, 63; aggressive
  tendering in new market 53; awards
  to apprentices 40, **41**, 45, 56; build
  up of labour force 25; Business
  Development Director 48-9; company's
  first lorry **13**; continues to grow 24-5;
  contracts worth £14 million 44; early
  estimate and successful tender 11; end
  of first ten years trading 23; fall of
  overall workload (1990-91) 53; first
  employee 41; first job 10; first
  marketing effort **11**; incorporated
  (1961) 7, 9; market share 53; motto,
  'Building a Greater London' 38, 41;
  new headquarters 43, 44; number
  and size of jobs in public sector 15;
  problems (1966) 14; profile 33, 57;
  profits 11, 13, 15, 41; second trading

year 13; system-built schools
  construction 27; turnover 11, 14, 16,
  28, 38, 41, 44, 45; twenty-first
  anniversary celebration 38, **39**
Higgins, Martin (son of Derek) 9, **13**,
  **56**; Group Board 60, 61; Hawke
  House site spotted by 43; joins
  Developments 38; Sales Director of
  Developments 45
Higgins, Olive (wife of Derek) 9, 39-41
  *passim*, 42, 46, 56, 63; hands over
  secretarial work to Gladys Smith 11;
  marriage to Derek 7
Higgins, Richard (son of Derek) 9, **13**,
  38, 43, 44, 48; Group Board 42, 46,
  47, 60, 61; increasingly interested
  in development business 34; joins
  company 26; Licentiate of the
  Institute of Builders 37; Managing
  Director of Developments 45
Higgins, Stephen (son of Derek) 9, **13**,
  **56**; joins company 38; Company
  Secretary of Developments 45; Group
  Board 47, 60, 61
HM Queen Elizabeth the Queen Mother
  33
Holley, Canon Jeffrey 44
Honor Oak 44
Horn Lane 8, 9, 16, 24, 25, 36; Building
  Works returned to 42; Higgins house
  11, **12**; filled to capacity 43; last
  photograph (1987) **17**; main office
  extended 26; office no longer big
  enough 13; original office demolished
  and replaced by Cumberland Court
  **44**; rear view showing offices and
  yard **12**; service for Gladys Smith 39
Hornchurch, Mitchell Junior School 17
Horvath, Robert 42, 46, 48, 60
Housing Corporation 62

Ilford 42; Borough Council 10;
  Goodmayes Library **31**; High Road
  36; Limewood Court sheltered
  housing scheme **21**; Little Heath ESN
  School 16; Nathan Sugar and Rita
  Simons Special Care Wing, Vi & John
  Rubens House 52, **53**; Investors in
  Industry Developments Limited 43
Islington **22**, 41, 43, 44, 45; Council 26,
  *49*; Mildmay Grove 34; Tibberton
  Square 35, 36

Jewish Welfare Board 53
John Grooms Housing Association 57
John J. Overy Partnership 52
Jupp, Graham 33

Kent, Duke of *41*
King, Benny 38, 47

Lambeth 56, **59**; West, Health
  Authority 63
Land and Urban PLC 44
Leonard Cheshire Foundation 44
Leonard, Miss (company's first
  customer) 10
Lever, John 57
Levitt Bernstein Associates 36, 58, 62
Lewisham 44
Leytonstone, Cann Hall Methodist
  Church 55
Liverpool Victoria (cricket club) 15
London 40; Bouverie Road 48; building
  to ease East End slum conditions 41;
  Covent Garden 42; Edward Henry
  House behind Coin Street 37, 38;
  Farrier Street 62; Hazelbourne
  Nursing Home 63; High Holborn 8;
  Mercedes Depot 30; new architectural
  commissions cancelled or postponed
  53; Pickford's Wharf 22, *49*;
  Richard's Place flats **19**; Savoy Hotel
  38, **39**; Shepherdess Walk 36; Stock
  Exchange 46, 48; West End 42, 47;
  Westwood Hill, The Fountain
  (hospice) **62**; *see also* City of London;
  Greater London; *also under individual
  borough names*
London & Quadrant Housing Trust 62
Longley, Bill 11
Look Ahead (Beacon Hostels) Housing
  Association Limited 43
Loughton 7, *32*, 34, 43, 47
Lovering, Bill 34

Matching Green Cricket Club 27
Matchroom Limited 52
MEB Partnership **54**
MEPK Architects **41**

Metro Properties Limited **20**
Metropolitan Police 13, 37
Midland Bank 8, 13, 42
Miller, Anne 52
Moran, Alan 40, 47
Mutter, Jim 28, 47

National Federation of Building Trades
  Employers 40, 45, 56; Building
  Together **59**
New Islington & Hackney Housing
  Association 48
Newham 34, 49
Newman VC, Col. Charles 8
Noble, Col. Sir Arthur 8, 39
Norris, Steven *52*
North Peckham, Gloucester Grove 60
North Weald Aerodrome *52*
Norwich Union Life Assurance Group
  42
Notting Hill, Harrow Road 60

Old Loughtonians Hockey Club 27, **61**
Oliff, Jim 17
Ongar 45

Pardey, Bill 9, 10, 13, 39, 41
Pardey, Olive *see* Higgins, Olive
Pearl Assurance 42
Pearlman Moiret Associates 51, 55
Penman, Barry 28, 38
Phoenix Trust **62**
Polygram UK Limited **22**, 52
Ponders End 43
Poplar 26
Price, Don 24, 45
Princes Park Avenue 36-7
Property Services Agency 47

Rainham **18**, 23, 24, 27
Rawlins, Jeff 47
Redbridge **16**, 23, 24, **31**
Rees, Merlyn 36
Rolls-Royce 10
Romford **22**, 24

Sabin, Bryan 47, 48-9
Sainsbury (J.) Limited 13
Sheppard (A. R.) 25
Sidney Kaye Firmin **53**
Sieff, Lord 52
Sisters of Charity of St Vincent de Paul
  29
Smith, Gladys 11, 13, 14, 39
Society of Co-Operative Dwellings 37
South Loughton 15
South West Essex Technical College 7
Southwark 45, 47
Sports Council **61**
Stapleford Aerodrome 11
Stepney 41, 43
Stratford 45
Sugar, Alan 52, **53**

Thomas, George 33
Tilbury 24
Tooley & Foster Partnership, The 7, **30**
Toomer, Leslie 17
Tooting 45
Tower Hamlets 49; Bethnal Green
  Estate **51**
Trustee Savings Bank 42
Tucker, Mr (bank manager) 8

Ujima Housing Association 62
Upton Park 52

Vancouver Trophy 33

Waltham Abbey, King Harold
  Secondary School 26
Waltham Cross 43
Waltham Forest **19**, 25, 50
Walthamstow 24, 26, 41, 43; Kestrel
  Court 38; Technical College 7, 8
Wanstead 10, 16, 13, 44, **51**, 57
Webster, Colin 8
Webster, Robert 8
White, Dick 38
White and Mileson 38, 43
Wilkinson, Walter 33
Wilson, Roger 60
Winged Fellowship (charity) **46**
Witham 8
Woodford Bridge 33
Woodford Green 9, 10, 26, 27, 33, 34

Young, Lord 52